Crypto Quick Guide

A step by step guide starting with your first-time Cryptocurrency Wallet Setup. This guide will get you up and running and will teach you how to create a wallet, buy Cryptocurrency, transfer Cryptocurrency, and sell Cryptocurrency. Lastly, we'll show you how to convert your Cryptocurrency back to fiat currency and transfer back to your bank.

DISCLAIMER:

***REMEMBER- THIS GUIDE IS NOT RECOMMENDING YOU BUY, SELL, OR TRADE ETHEREUM OR ANY OTHER CRYPTOCURRENCIES OR NFTS. WE ARE NOT FINANCIAL ADVISORS. WE ARE NOT RESPONSIBLE FOR ANY LOSS YOU MAY INCUR BY INVESTING YOUR MONEY INTO THE CRYPTO OR NFT MARKET. THE SOLE PURPOSE OF THIS GUIDE IS TO SIMPLY AND EASILY BREAK DOWN THE STEPS TO SET UP YOUR CRYPTO WALLET AND USE THE FUNCTIONS ON THE COINBASE AND METAMASK APPLICATIONS. THIS GUIDE USES ETHEREUM AS THE CRYPTOCURRENCY OF CHOICE TO SHARE WHAT EACH STEP LOOKS LIKE WHEN BUYING, SELLING, AND TRANSFERRING ETHEREUM. NOTE THAT USING THESE SAME STEPS WITH A DIFFERENT FORM OF CRYPTOCURRENCY INSTEAD OF ETHEREUM MAY LEAD TO LOSS OF YOUR CRYPTO, AS THESE STEPS ARE SPECIFIC TO ETHEREUM. ALWAYS CONSULT WITH A FINANCIAL PROFESSIONAL BEFORE BUYING, SELLING, OR SENDING ANY CRYPTOCURRENCY OR NFTS. THE METHODS, PLATFORMS, CRYPTOCURRENCIES, NFTS, AND STEPS THAT WE DISCUSS AND USE WITHIN THIS GUIDE ARE NOT THE ONLY EXISTING METHODS OR ASSETS THAT EXIST. THEY ARE THE METHODS, PLATFORMS, AND ASSETS THAT WE HAVE FOUND TO BE THE EASIEST FOR FIRST TIME USERS, AND THE ONES THAT WE HAVE CHOSEN TO USE FOR EXAMPLES WITHIN THIS GUIDE. ALWAYS D.Y.O.R. (DO YOUR OWN RESEARCH).

Let's get into it!

The first thing you'll need to make your first Cryptocurrency purchase is a Cryptocurrency Exchange app. We will use Coinbase. Follow below...

STEP 1:

On the App Store, download the Coinbase app. Do not confuse with the Coinbase WALLET app.

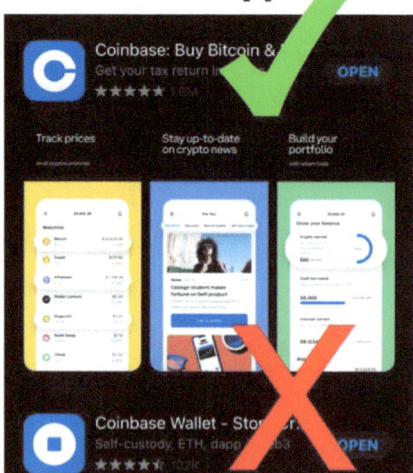

ONCE THE APP DOWNLOAD IS COMPLETE, MOVE ONTO STEP 2-

First, you'll need to fund your Coinbase account with either a Credit/Debit Card or a Bank Account. Follow below..

STEP 2:

Once you've created an account on Coinbase, go to your profile and settings, and then choose the method in which you'd like to fund your account.

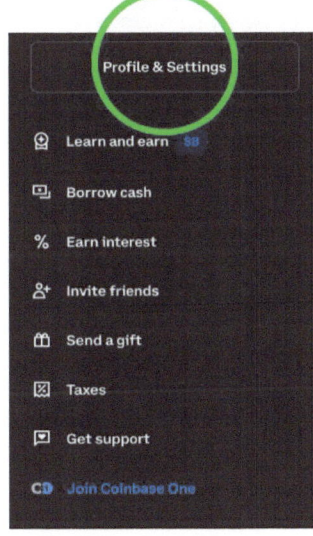

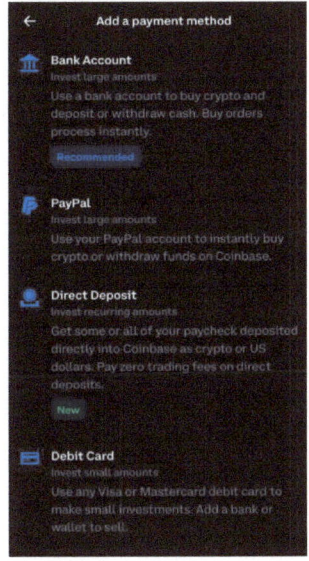

NOT AFFILIATED IN ANY WAY WITH COINBASE, METAMASK, OPENSEA, OR ANY PLATFORMS MENTIONED WITHIN

Here, you'll transfer the amount of money that you'd like to get started investing in Cryptocurrency with.

A quick note:

This tutorial will show you how to purchase and send ETHEREUM. Prior to investing in Ethereum or any other Cryptocurrency, it is crucial that you understand that the prices of Cryptocurrencies can fluctuate dramatically. HOWTOCRYPTO.ME is not providing ANY financial advice. Instead, HOWTOCRYPTO.ME is providing a guide for those who've done their Due diligence on the risks of investing in cryptocurrency and who've consulted with a financial professional on the risks of investing in cryptocurrency.

Moving along..

After you've selected your payment method on Coinbase:

On the Coinbase homepage, select Ethereum.

ONCE YOU'VE SELECTED ETHEREUM (Which you will see frequently abbreviated as ETH), continue below.

ONCE YOU'VE SELECTED ETHEREUM ON THE COINBASE HOMEPAGE:

To purchase Ethereum with your linked payment method, click "Trade"

Here, you're able to purchase as much or as little Ethereum as you'd like ⟶

This is where you will buy as much or as little Ethereum (ETH) as you'd like. You can enter any dollar amount that you'd like to spend and you will receive the equivalent amount in ETH. For example, if the price of Ethereum is $3500 today, then spending $3500 will get you 1 ETH. If you don't want to buy an entire ETH, don't worry. For example, if you buy $150 worth of Ethereum with 1 ETH being worth $3500, you'd receive approximately .04 ETH as opposed to 1 ETH. There is no amount too large or too small.

ONCE YOU'VE COMPLETED YOUR ETHEREUM PURCHASE ON
COINBASE, HEAD BACK TO THE APP STORE. (Or the Google Chrome
Store if you're on a laptop or desktop)

STEP 3:

**If you are using a mobile phone, go back to the App
Store and download the METAMASK app. If you
you'd prefer to store your crypto assets on a
computer, go to https://metamask.io/ and
download the METAMASK chrome extension.**

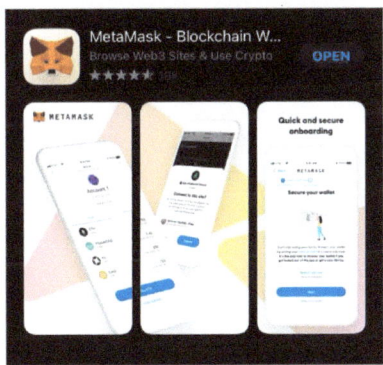

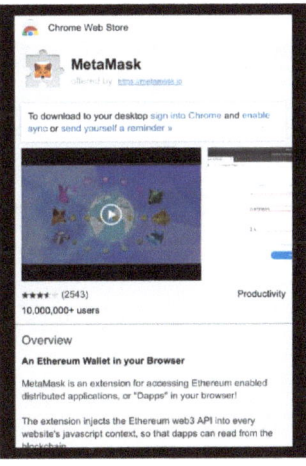

**ONCE YOU'VE INSTALLED THE METAMASK APP ON YOUR PHONE OR THE
METAMASK CHROME EXTENSION ON YOUR COMPUTER, CONTINUE BELOW..**

STEP 3 (cont.) :

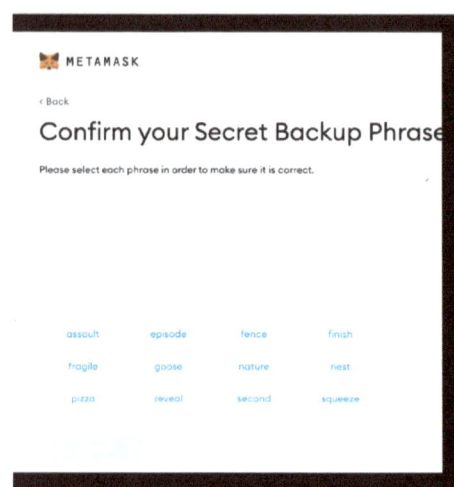

Open Metamask and select the prompt to create a new wallet. Once you are directed to the page that shows your secret recovery phrase composed of either 12 or 24 random words, be sure to write that down on paper. You can also write it on metal or some other durable and safe surface where you can hide it somewhere and keep it safe. Do not ever share this phrase with ANYBODY ELSE. It is the only way you will be able to recover your assets and if somebody else gets this phrase or if it gets lost then you will lose access to your cryptocurrency and other digital assets and they will not be recoverable. Never store this phrase anywhere on your electronic devices, as they can be hacked or stolen.

ONCE YOU'VE <u>WRITTEN AND SAFELY STORED</u> YOUR SEED PHRASE, MOVE ONTO THE NEXT STEP-

....NOW THAT YOU'VE SAFELY WRITTEN AND STORED YOUR 12 OR 24 WORD SEED-PHRASE, OPEN UP THE METAMASK APP ON YOUR PHONE OR IN YOUR GOOGLE CHROME BROWSER..

STEP 4 :

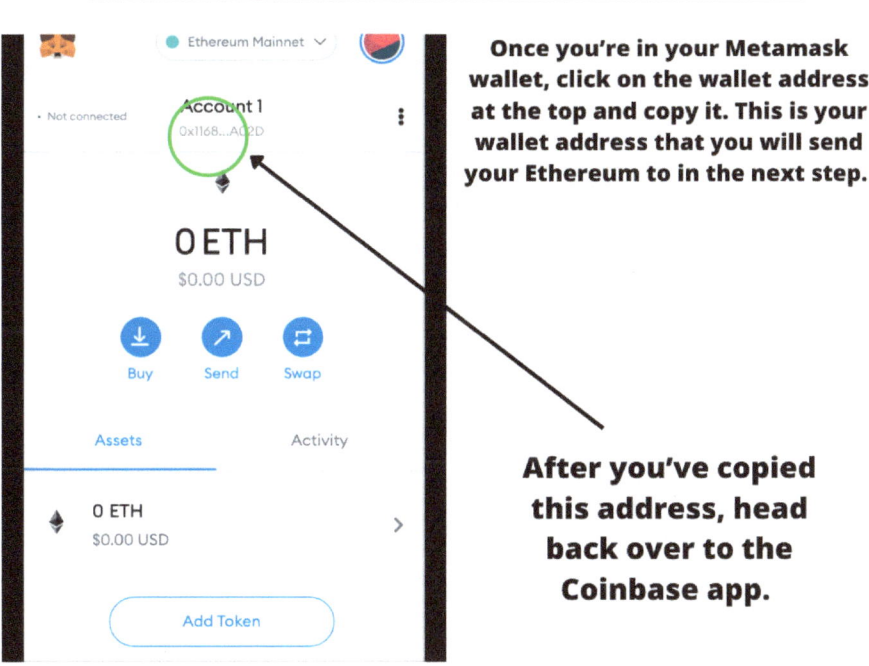

Once you're in your Metamask wallet, click on the wallet address at the top and copy it. This is your wallet address that you will send your Ethereum to in the next step.

After you've copied this address, head back over to the Coinbase app.

ONCE YOU'VE CLICKED AND COPIED YOUR WALLET ADDRESS IN METAMASK, GO BACK INTO YOUR COINBASE APP WHERE YOU FIRST PURCHASED YOUR ETHEREUM IN STEP 1.

STEP 4 (cont'):

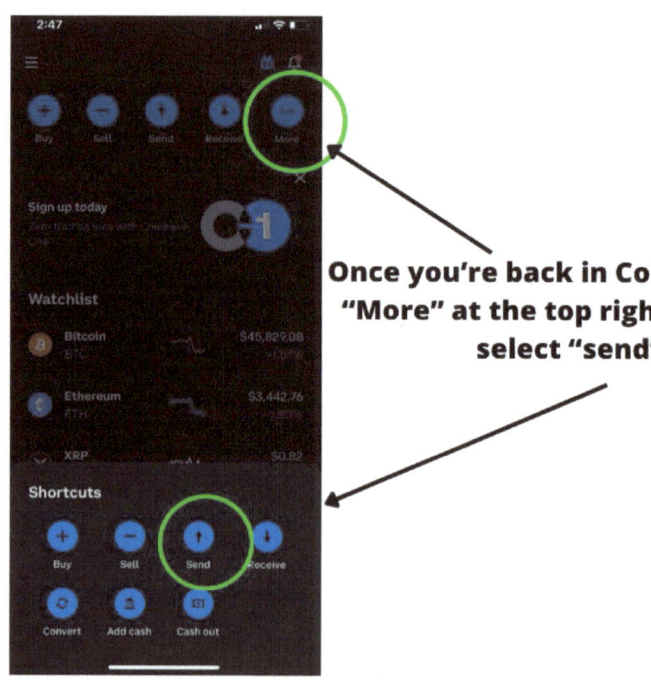

Once you're back in Coinbase, click "More" at the top right, and then select "send".

STEP 4 (cont'):

Select Ethereum, and then choose the amount you'd like to send to your Metamask wallet. Click continue. Think of your Metamask wallet as sort of a savings account to keep larger amounts of crypto, and your Coinbase app as sort of a checking account to keep less on.

NOTE**

For now- only send Ethereum to your Metamask Wallet. If you'd like to send Bitcoin or other cryptocurrencies down the line there is a separate step to import those into Metamask. We will only cover sending Ethereum today.

STEP 4 (cont'):

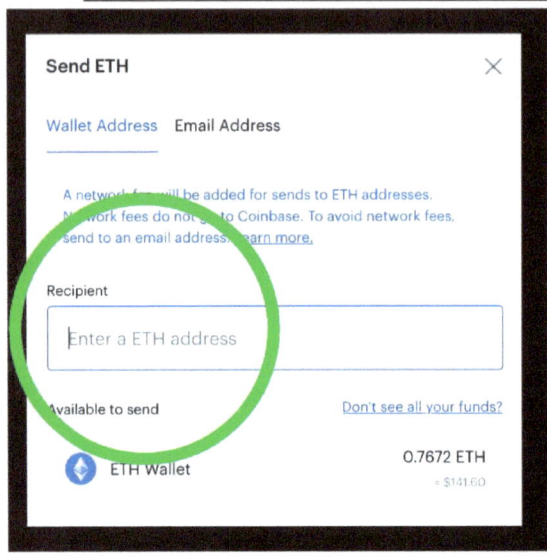

Click next until you reach the recipient page. (Your screen may look a bit different depending on which device you're on.)

In the recipient box, it is now time to PASTE the address from Metamask that we copied in the last step.

STEP 4 (cont'):

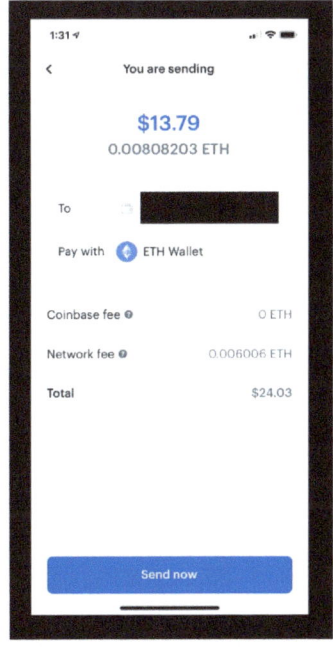

Verify the address that you are sending to matches the one on your Metamask account up at the top that we copied before.

You will now be able to click send, and send your Ethereum to your Metamask wallet.

Be patient, it can take up to 15 minutes in some cases for the Ethereum to show up in your Metamask

NOT AFFILIATED IN ANY WAY WITH COINBASE, METAMASK, OPENSEA, OR ANY PLATFORMS MENTIONED WITHIN

ONCE YOU'VE HIT "SEND NOW" IN COINBASE, GO BACK INTO YOUR METAMASK WALLET AND WAIT UNTIL YOU SEE THE ETHEREUM SHOW UP THERE. THIS WILL TAKE A FEW MINUTES. BE PATIENT AND DO NOT PANIC IF IT TAKES LONGER THAN EXPECTED. ONCE IT SHOWS UP IN YOUR METAMASK ACCOUNT, HEAD TO THE NEXT STEP-

ONCE THE TRANSFER IS COMPLETE-

You sent your Ethereum from your Coinbase app to your Metamask Wallet. What's next?

Your Metamask wallet should now look something like this:

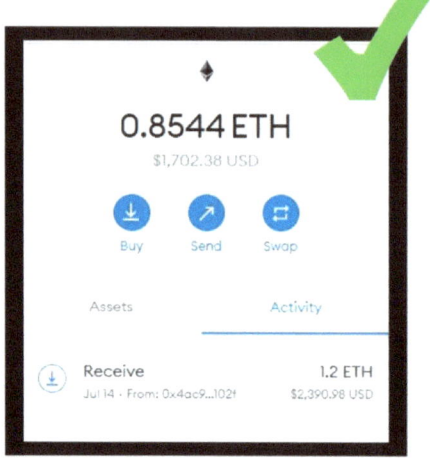

ONCE YOU SEE YOUR ETH BALANCE IN YOUR METAMASK WALLET, YOU'VE COMPLETED YOUR BASIC WALLET SETUP AND FUNDING! YOUR COINBASE APP IS WHERE YOU'LL PURCHASE CRYPTOCURRENCY AND YOUR METAMASK WALLET IS WHERE YOU'LL SEND IT TO SAFELY STORE IT. CONTINUE BELOW TO SEE HOW TO CASH OUT BACK TO YOUR BANK.

WHAT'S NEXT?

**NOTE: The following steps are not necessarily intended to be completed right now. They are here for your reference for when you'd like to cash out your ETH back to your bank account. Feel free to refer back to this guide at any time.

CASHING OUT TO YOUR BANK

For reference- this is how you'll cash out any crypto back to your bank account.

1) OPEN COINBASE

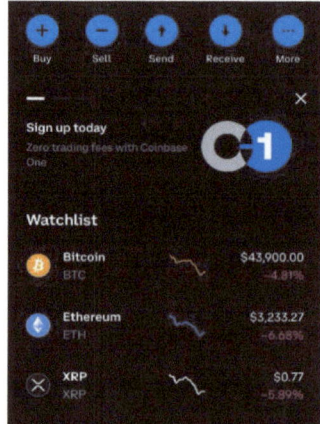

NEXT,

CASHING OUT TO YOUR BANK

For reference- this is how you'll cash out any crypto back to your bank account.

2) SELECT "RECEIVE"

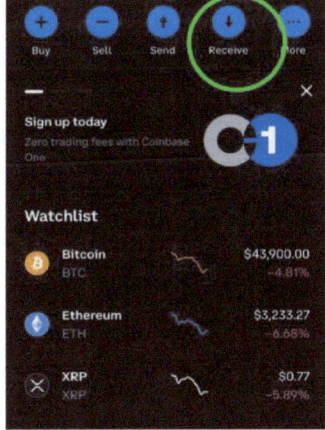

CASHING OUT TO YOUR BANK

For reference- this is how you'll cash out any crypto back to your bank account.

3) Select "Receive Ethereum" and click COPY next to the address

AFTER YOU'VE COPIED YOUR **ETHEREUM** ADDRESS IN COINBASE (VERIFY YOU'VE COPIED YOUR **ETHEREUM** ADDRESS AND NOT ANY OTHER CRYPTO ADDRESS OTHERWISE YOU WILL LOSE THE ETHEREUM THAT YOU ARE TRYING TO SEND.), CONTINUE BELOW:

CASHING OUT TO YOUR BANK

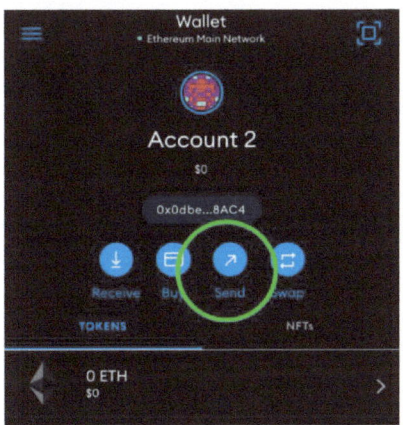

4) Now go back to your Metamask wallet and select "Send"

5) In the "To" field, paste the address we just copied in Coinbase.

Paste your Ethereum address that we just copied from Coinbase in the "To" field.

Enter the amount you'd like to send back to Coinbase to cash out.

CASHING OUT TO YOUR BANK

...Enter in the amount of Ethereum that you'd like to cash out, and hit send.

...After a few minutes you'll see the Ethereum Balance show up in your Coinbase. Be patient, it may take up to 10 minutes.

After you've hit SEND in Metamask, head back to your Coinbase App.

CASHING OUT TO YOUR BANK

Once the Ethereum balance shows up in your Coinbase account, click on Ethereum in Coinbase.

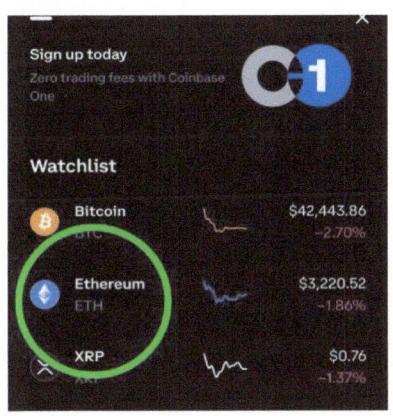

(IT WILL TAKE UP TO 10 MINUTES TO SHOW UP IN YOUR COINBASE ACCOUNT. BE PATIENT!)

ONCE THE ETHEREUM SHOWS UP IN YOUR COINBASE, CLICK ON ETHEREUM ON THE COINBASE HOMEPAGE.

Cashing out from Crypto
back to your bank

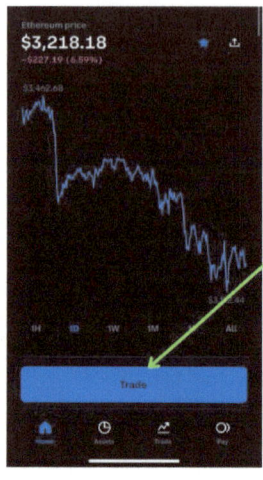

First, click "Trade"

Next, click "sell ETH"

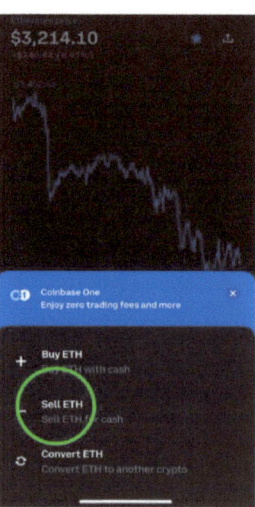

NOT AFFILIATED IN ANY WAY WITH COINBASE, METAMASK, OPENSEA, OR ANY PLATFORMS MENTIONED WITHIN

Cashing out from Crypto back to your bank

Once you've sold your Ethereum, click "More" at the top right, and then select "Cash Out"

...FROM HERE YOU WILL BE ABLE TO SELECT THE BANK ACCOUNT IN WHICH YOU'D LIKE TO CASH OUT TO.

CONGRATS!! You've completed your basic wallet setup and learned how to buy, transfer, and sell Cryptocurrency.

End course.